ARTWORK
ON THE BACKS of GARGOYLES

a collection of Villanelles and Sestinas
(and a pair of paradelles)

by

LYN COFFIN

TRANSCENDENT ZERO PRESS
HOUSTON, TEXAS

ISBN-13: 978-1-946460-31-8
Library of Congress Control Number: 2021938866

Printed in the United States of America

Transcendent Zero Press
16429 El Camino Real Apt. #7
Houston, TX 77062

Cover photo: Column Capital at St. Pierre in Chauvigny, taken by Walt Halperin

Cover design by Nino Chavchavadze

FIRST EDITION

PRAISE FOR
THE ARTWORK ON THE BACKS of GARGOYLES

Lyn Coffin wields words in these exacting forms with a keen ferocity that sets our darknesses shining. These elegant language lattices hold, and hold forth for us, Coffin's X-ray images of love's underside. Her villanelles, sestinas, and paradelles are tender and wicked, sincere and teasing—they laugh at us, cry for us, accuse, and forgive.

I've followed Lyn Coffin's writing for many years, and reading Artworks on the Backs of Gargoyles, I recognize the long-seasoned craft, wit, and heart necessary for the creation of such work. Her voice, in layered harmonics, invites us into a music that is not only American or contemporary—she sings for the ages, before and beyond.

This collection is amazing work! It's downright timelessly kick-ass.

   —Jed Myers, author of *The Marriage of Space and Time* and *Watching the Perseids*

In 'Artwork on the Backs of Gargoyles,' Lyn Coffin, poet, novelist and translator, proves herself a master of the poetic forms, the villanelle, the sestina, and the paradelle, in which she casts both an empathic and a sardonic eye on the internal lives of damaged, cruel, tender, passionate, dispassionate, and above all, haunting men, women and children.

Her organization of poems, in male, female, and gender-fluid voices, leads to a coda of some more openly autobiographical pieces in their contemplations of love, life and death, ending in "Mother's Note Home," with the line, "Whatever light describes, the dark embraces." As she embraces the daily, dream-like, and seminal moments of life in these finely crafted poems, Lyn Coffin gives us captivating artwork on the backs of gargoyles.

   —Joanne Ward, author of *Utility*

Written in both male and female voices, Artwork on the Backs of Gargoyles is a rich journey through birth and death, love and loss, filled with magic, mystery and the mythical dark. Lyn Coffin explores the longing for our animal nature alongside the conundrum of our sexual nature and the challenges of love. A bounty of images, this collection of villanelles and sestinas moves the reader "through hills that rise like music and fall like rain". The poet asks "...if it makes/ The same noise as angels liquid in the steel/ Tines of sunlight....". Yes, it does.

— Mary Eliza Crane, author of *What I Can Hold in My Hands* and *At First Light*

Writing about love, like writing about nature, is almost impossible: the reader's fashioning of the ideal is forced through the prism of the writer and becomes a subject for rejection. Whatever we write seems trivial when compared with nature or love.

Love poems must incorporate two seemingly disparate elements, the spiritual and the carnal. It's a rare poem that can unite both. Many of the poems in The Artwork on the Backs of Gargoyles are love poems which do just that: they reach "wuthering heights," and can be gladly received by readers who are not weighed down by either the spiritual or the carnal.

— Leszek Chudzinski, author of *Sunday Morning Poets*

In her lifetime, Elizabeth Bishop published a mere brace of emblematic sestinas and a single, monumental villanelle, and she never wrote any paradelles. To this One Art, Lyn Coffin proffers her *Artwork on the Backs of Gargoyles*, comprised of a few dozen villanelles and sestinas, and a couple of paradelles. In this collection, drawn from earlier books of Coffin's as well as from more recent manuscripts, I am most taken with the nonce variations on these forms. The title poem, for example, is a "*septina*" with successively dropping end-words, rather like a prosodic variation on musical chairs; and the pair, possibly nesting, of paradelles is mischievously elusive, playing a sort of poetic hide-and-seek with the reader. Kudos to Coffin! – I thoroughly enjoyed these artful poems, even without a gargoyle at my back."

— Carolyne Wright, author of *Masquerade* and *This Dream the World: New & Selected Poems*

It is always a treat to read what Lyn Coffin has written because she writes in so many genres and so inventively. Here she demonstrates a command of sestina variations, of villanelles, and of the paradelle. Coffin excels in presenting fantasy and the macabre. Her riffs on colloquialisms are word play delights, as are her rhymes, enjambments, and metaphors. Riddles abound in this engaging collection-- "I have buried the hatchet in my lovers"-- and her work benefits from reading and rereading.

— Mary Ellen Talley, author of *Postcards from the Lilac City*

Lyn Coffin undertakes two of the most daunting formal challenges of Western poetic tradition: the villanelle and sestina—forms alternating throughout this sequence of forty-nine poems. The first third of them in "Male Voices" shows men responding to all kinds of relationships. The next third, "Female Voices," has various feminine speakers. In the last section, "Love," the author speaks in her own person. Many poems tell a story. The overall effect is a human comedy in verse, and virtually all the speakers have something emotionally important at stake. While observing the usual constraints of the forms, the author also explores such variations as the "bike-lock" and rhymed sestina. The book is a masterful demonstration of passionate versatility.

— Edward Morin, author of three poetry collections and co-translator of *The Red Azalea: Chinese Poetry since the Cultural Revolution*

ARTWORK
ON THE BACKS of GARGOYLES

a collection of Villanelles and Sestinas
(and a pair of paradelles)

by

LYN COFFIN

ARTWORK ON THE BACKS of GARGOYLES
a brief introduction

As performance poetry (spoken word, slam, hip-hop) takes center stage in this 21st century moment, it's a brave poet indeed who not only turns to the structured schemes of earlier times, but who presents an entire book in two of the most demanding forms: the sestina and the villanelle. Lyn Coffin is such a brave poet.

Her brilliant manipulation of rhyme, metaphor, narrative and imagery—crammed into the beautiful rhyming prisons of repetitive structures—intensifies her subjects until they glow, bleed, and cry aloud.

Coffin focuses her attention on the voices of suffering and the suffering of the voiceless, from Oedipus Rex to the Wild Boy of Aveyron; from Rapunzel to a teacher trying to lure her students into language. Because the long sestina form is for telling stories and the short, repetitive villanelle is best at telling feelings, Coffin's technique cleverly covers the two poles of poetry—narrative and passion. Together they transform the familiar into the strange, erotic, and surprising.

Her fascinating characters fill the pages of this collection with subtle and dire tales as they navigate a baffling and dangerous world. The collection is divided into three sections focused on Male Voices, Female Voices, and Gender-Fluid Voices (Love).

Suffering is met with bafflement and passivity in "Another Country" in which a Male Voice tells us that:

"…Our marriage was like a country
whose borders had been closed; the terrain was smooth,
but there were bread lines, men who vanished, foreign
soldiers directing traffic… It was dangerous to relax."

In the Female section, Coffin ratchets up Rapunzel's familiar anguish of isolation to life-threatening peril: "Lost in separateness, I sometimes forget/ where I am. The witch's minions stand sentry/ at every open window." But in the next stanza Rapunzel discovers a larger, more dangerous world: "There may be no blue numbers on my arm, yet/the storm is closing in. There's a black Nazi/ at every window."

Coffin adds to her poetic hurdles a third form, the paradelle, which is so repetitive that the poet is restricted to the convoluted re-use of line after line—a structure, that strangely suits those emotions in which the hamster of suffering can do little more than run and rerun the wheel of grief. Even here, she manages variation. In "Dying in the Hospital" the persona says "You lie mute, and don't manage to look at me./ You look at me, and don't manage to lie mute." And later: "Nothing means anything to me now; we are a bell without sound./ We are a bell without sound now; nothing means anything to me."

Coffin's daring, brilliant poems use the most restrictive forms to deliver the most expansive meditations on the ordeals of living. Not for her the talky sing-song of the current moment. Her poems jump high hurdles-- and deliver deep and satisfying rewards.

— Sharon Cumberland, author of *Peculiar Honors,* and *Strange With Age*

for Gala

A few of the poems in The Artwork on the Backs of Gargoyles *appeared in previous books.*

These poems are listed following the name of the book in which they first appeared:

BOOKS OF POETRY:

Human Trappings (Oedipus and the Sphinx)
The Poetry of Wickedness (A Life)
Crystals of the Unforeseen (Intro to Lit)
East and West, with Bavudorj Tsog
Joseph Brodsky Was Joseph Brodsky (A Door that Doesn't Exist)
A Marriage Without Consummation, with Givi Alkhazishvili
Of Rifles and Reception Lines, with Mercedes Luna Fuentes
This Green Life (Paradelle on Love and *Ned's Aria)*

BOOKS OF POETRY in Translation

მე ორი ვარ, (Georgian)
როდენის შეყვარებული, (Georgian)
La Vida Verde, (Spanish)

BOOKS OF TRANSLATION

Elegies, Jiří Orten
The Plague Monument, Jaroslav Seifert
Poetry, Anna Akhmatova
More than One Life, Miloslava Holubova
White Picture, Jiří Orten
Georgian Poetry, Rustaveli to Galaktion
Animalarky, Zaza Abiadnidze
Islands in the Stream of Time, Germain Droogenbroodt
Still Life with Snow, Dato Barbakadze (with Nato Alhazishvili)
The Adventures of a Boy Named Piccolo, Archil Sulakauri
The Knight in the Panther Skin, Shota Rustaveli
Standing on Earth, Mohsen Emadi

The Adventures of a Boy Named Piccolo, Archil Sulakauri
Baratashvili, Nikoloz Baratashvili (English translation)
Aphorisms, Shota Rustaveli
Three Centuries of Georgian Poetry (Baratashvili, Galaktion, Barbakadze)
Sunday Poets, Leszek Z. Chudzinski
Poetry of Razhden Gvetadze (forthcoming)

BOOKS OF FICTION

The First Honeymoon (short stories)
The Aftermath (a novel)

DRAMA COLLECTIONS

A Taste of Cascadia
10 x 10, with Natalya Churlyaeva, in English and Russian

Lyn's work has appeared in many anthologies and over 100 small magazines and literary reviews, including Time magazine.

PART ONE: *Male Voices*

PART TWO: *Female Voices*

CODA: *Gender-Fluid Voices* (Love)

PART ONE:
MALE VOICES

THE SCREEN, THE SCAFFOLD

A small Italian museum of art.
A parquet floor streaked with sunlight.
A glassed-in display case where one can see
a small antique decorated screen
used long ago by priests who sometimes
walked with the condemned as far as the scaffold,

and blocked the criminal's view of the scaffold
with the screen, distracting him with art
as long as humanly possible. Sometimes
the screen had a scene of birds and sunlight,
sometimes there was just a tree on the screen.
Sometimes the only thing to see

was a child. Maybe the condemned could see
in that child his childhood's trip towards the scaffold.
The happy smile of the boy on the screen
would then be more painful because of its art
than what there was *really*-- the walk in sunlight,
the minutes tick-tocking. Sometimes,

he looked past the screen. Sometimes
he wanted to see real birds, to see
a moving speck in the sky, in the sunlight,
or people lining the road to the scaffold.
He might have felt sickened by fastidious art,
the bird or the tree or the child on the screen

delicate enough to have been the screen
of a childhood victim. He must sometimes
have wondered whether the purpose of art
was to distract him from what others could see:
the steps, the kneeling block, the scaffold,
a hooded man, something reflecting sunlight.

He mounted the scaffold, slow in the sunlight,
and stumbled his way without a screen
to the man at the center of the scaffold
standing haloed.... We weep because sometimes
in images meant to distract, we can see
the awful truth, grinning in a mask of art,

but sometimes art on a painted screen
will postpone the seeing of the scaffold,
and sunlight glancing off the blade of the axe.

THIS GAY LIFE*

That's more like it, I finally heard him say-
I'd do without the forceps if I could.
As I relaxed, I felt the world give way.

At ten, I slipped out after dark to play.
Father didn't hit me, though he thought he should.
That's more like it, I finally heard him say.

At twenty, I had a stage lover. I lay
shaking in his arms in a backstage wood.
As I relaxed, I felt the world give way.

We "married." For ten years, he managed to stay
faithful. When he erred, I said I understood.
That's more like it, I finally heard him say.

At forty, beds got blanketed with gray.
I wanted to die peacefully if I could.
As I relaxed, I felt the world give way.

I dream of God, discover I can pray,
can be obedient for my own good.
That's more like it, I finally hear Him say.
As I relax, I feel the world give way.

this is a "present" villanelle, where the tense changes in the final line

RIDERLESS HORSES

He stood on the shore in a circle of ruins
recalling the words of the lady in white:
"If you manage to waylay the magical children
as they ride to the ocean through their ominous country,
and make certain your lips never touch any salt,
the secret they tell you will save you from drowning…"

He dreaded the thought that he might die by drowning
and began to revise his view of the ruins.
He scraped a stone table encrusted with salt
and discovered words that were filled in with white:
"Here lies the king of an alien country,
challenged and murdered by magical children."

As the shadows grew long in the land of the children,
he wondered what words might save him from drowning:
he remembered tales that were told of this country,
that Satan had made of God's city these ruins,
turned the moon clumsy, a crony in white,
and scattered stars on the night sky like salt.

He kept himself steady by thinking of salt.
Suddenly he was surrounded by children,
weaving a circle of pale gold and white.
Then he grew unafraid and forgot about drowning.
Now as he stood in the center of ruins,
he looked like a king from an alien country:

"Children, I've come to your perilous country,
where the moon's like a stone and the stones are like salt,
to learn why you ride to the sea through these ruins."
Clearer than water came the words of the children:
"Tomorrow's the day set for trial by drowning."
They brought him a mantle, vermilion and white,

Led him to the shore where a woman in white
pronounced him the king of the magical country,
and prepared him for dawn, for the trial by drowning...
He strode through the water, lips flagrant with salt,
and they followed as one, the woman and children,
leaving riderless horses to stray through the ruins.

For the woman in white and the magical children,
drownings are doors: they returned to their ruins.
The man was left settled in the country of salt.

SLEEPING PRINCE: THE WILD BOY OF AVEYRON

January, 1800. A naked
boy crept out of the French woods, scooped fresh water
from a ditch, dug potatoes, then made quick work
of eating. He paid no heed as they closed in,
but at the first touch, fought being taken
with the soundless, whirling fury of a dream.

Those who caught him were untouched by any dream
of knowledge: it was just wrong for a naked
boy to run wild. Their town had always taken
morals to heart. They gave him clothes, food, water,
spoke of release. But progress closed in
on him: historical forces were at work.

A scientist named Itard began to work
with the boy-- A brilliant man, fueled by a dream
of freeing the humanity enclosed in
that bestial husk, revealing the naked
mind. The boy seemed to want only food, water,
sleep: he might learn to speak if these were taken

from him. Itard didn't know what he'd taken
upon himself. After years of hard work,
the boy was toilet-trained, wore clothes, drank water
from a cup, but the original dream--
to make a civilized man from a naked
boy-- was abandoned: time and silence closed in.

The boy was better about being closed in.
He dressed himself, kept clean, liked being taken
in hand by women. Still, he slept naked
and touched girls who came to help with the work
in ways that violated their common dream
of love. He ate like a beast, but drank water

like a saint: he could knife through the dark water
of mountain lakes from dawn until night closed in.
They gave him, still mute, to a woman whose dream
was to have a son. After he'd been taken,
Itard said he'd first known the boy was his life's work
when he saw him sleeping, dreamless and naked.

No kisses work. The prince stays closed in ice. Still--
in wild dreams of bright water, a naked boy
leaps free, laughs, and will not be overtaken.

MEMENTO*

Remember me, mother-- I'm the son who
dreams of my sister on cold nights. I dream she
is dying in your arms. It's all I can do

to keep from kissing her thin wrists and ice-blue
lips. She plays cats-paw, which is how she
remembers me, mother. I'm the son who

dreams of a wife. She loses her glass slipper
but hardly has the coach turned pumpkin than she
is dying in your arms. It's all I can do

to keep from kissing her breasts. Her breasts are two
grenades in tapioca: that's why she
remembers me, mother. I'm the son who

dreams of your husband, mother. He careens through
the room, and jumps from my high window. Soon he
is dying in your arms. It's all I can do

to keep from kissing you. You suspect me
for the right reason: I can't stop loving you.
Remember me, mother. I'm the son who
is dying in your arms. It's all I can do.

*this is the first of a few "switched" villanelles: the final stanza is ordered
b/a/a/a instead of the normal a/b/a/a

26

OEDIPUS AND THE SPHINX

He stopped in mid-stride. Her blue-flame eyes were so
pure they made him recall childhood-- long
days spent with shepherds in the mountains near home.
While the sheep grazed like clouds that had found their legs,
he lay back, amazed that his royal body
could so adapt itself to the common ground.

Now it was all he could do to stand his ground:
her eyes reduced past and future to so
much ash, so much wood to burn. Her body
seemed puzzled together: china-doll face, long
snowy wings, woman's breasts; the trunk, tail and legs
of she-lions. She was keeping him from home--

from the city he'd chosen as his new home.
While he watched, she lowered herself to the ground,
tucked her little-girl face between those hind legs
and sniffed the blood that leaked from her like so
much milk. She licked her soft gray parts a long
time and nosed over the rest of her body.

A sour-milk smell came from her body.
Something-- not fear-- made him sorry he'd left home.
The priests had delivered themselves of a long,
tedious lecture: "Be silent. Stand your ground,"
they'd said. "If you try speaking first, as so
many men have done, she'll sprout two more legs

from her belly and, using those new legs
like arms, strangle you, then tear your body
into small pieces as though it were so
much soft bread. If you want to reach your new home,
wait for her riddle." He stood his ground
until his bad foot seemed on fire from the long

ordeal. The sun was setting and the long
day nearly done when, head snaking from her legs,
she asked the riddle. He sank to the ground
and shouted out the answer. Her body
shaking, she waited for his sword to strike home.
Later, some claimed his answer killed her. Not so.

From the ground, he thrust his long sword home,
between her legs. Her body might have survived that. So
he'd poisoned the blade with his father's blood.

THE BREAKFAST NOOK

The bombardier's medals are thorns in his chest:
He faces his son across the breakfast nook.
Back to the wall, he smiles and forgets the rest

of what he meant to say. "Is war like a test?"
his son asks. How to answer that trusting look?
The bombardier's medals are thorns in his chest.

Should he say, "I destroyed a machine gun nest?"
"I didn't die because I had what it took"?
Back to the wall, he smiles and forgets the rest

of his day. He's back flying over the west
of France, above quilted fields, stitched by a brook.
The bombardier's medals are thorns in his chest.

He's hit, bails out over Holland, thinks, "It's best
not to think ahead." They catch him in the Hook.
Back to the wall, he smiles and forgets the rest

of the war.... The German squad goes by the book:
a year later, he's in the breakfast nook.
The bombardier's medals are thorns in his chest.
Back to the wall, he smiles, and forgets the rest.

*this is the first of many "couplet" villanelles in this collection: the final stanza
is b/b/a/a/ instead of the standard a/b/a/a.

THE ENDING END*

Beginnings, yes. But who knows how things will end?
A feverish child, bolt upright in his bed
doesn't, or his mother, forced to bend
over her own lap, biting off loose thread
as she sews. Most predators, muzzling fine
kills, think nothing of it. But men, who divine

water with forked sticks and think themselves divine
might well ask themselves: Who knows where things will end?
My Sunday school teachers didn't confine
themselves to prose: "Sing at table, Sing in bed,
Devil will get you, hang you up by a thread.
Wind sends boughs crashing, but virtue won't bend.

That's the end." The straight-and-narrow took a bend
when my high school art teacher praised "the divine
Fragonard... Classicism hung by a thread.
His swinging girl, her half-off shoe, marked the end
of it." I hung that picture above my bed:
I imagined looking up her dress, to fine

white panties. Taking them off, I saw her fine
cleft... I'd try more, find my finger wouldn't bend,
and wake to discover I'd wet the bed.
Mom said she didn't mind the wet sheets: "Divine
providence, they tell me, shapes every end,"
she joked with crinkled eyes, but then lost her thread

of thought... I put myself through college-- silk thread
through a steel needle. I discovered the fine
art of listening to music. One prof would end
his classes playing operas he thought would "bend
our ears, reintroduce us to the divine."
He said, "Rosenkavalier was the sickbed

30

where romanticism died." I sat in bed
that night, and let his words begin to thread
their way through my mind. They seemed to me divine
words, spoken from beyond the final confine--
time: they beckoned me around the last bend
of thought. I asked myself: "Who knows where things end?"

I realize, in fine, I'm mortal, not divine.
Winds blow, I bend. I don't know where things end.
Above my bed, a sword hangs by a thread.

this is a rhymed sestina

HIS FACE DARKENED

His face darkened like a cold field. He tightened
his tie. "My wife--" he muttered, shaking his head.
"I love her. But just because she's frightened

of what lurks in the night, she drags me to bed
while it's still light out." His wife's pale cheeks flared red.
His face darkened like a cold field. He tightened

his grip. "You go to bed with her instead,"
he proposed. I laughed..."I'm serious," he said.
"I love her, but just because she's frightened

of sex, she can't--" At this point, his wife fled
the room crying. Her husband looked almost dead.
His face darkened like a cold field. He tightened

his doorknob hand. "I want what I used to dread,"
he told me. "The drunk couplings of the ill-bred.
I love her, but just because she's frightened

of me, she won't...." He stopped, held up his hand, spread
his fingers. "I can't keep her hungers fed."
His face darkened. Like a cold field, he tightened.
"I love her, but just because she's frightened."

ANOTHER COUNTRY

The sun felt hot on our foreheads. A foreign
leader spoke for hours in uncontracted
English on the need to achieve easier
relations—(Beside me, my wife's smooth,
noncommittal face)—and efforts to relax
tensions. He said his country and our country

were alike. "Alike, hell. His so-called country
is a tribal mess," I whispered. The foreign
look my wife shot me made it hard to relax.
When I took her white hand, it first contracted
like a scared animal, then lay still and smooth
in my own. It struck me how much easier

unmarried life had been for me. Easier
for her, too. Our marriage was like a country
whose borders had been closed; the terrain was smooth,
but there were bread lines, men who vanished, foreign
soldiers directing traffic, uncontracted
disputes. It was dangerous to relax.

After the speech, my wife managed to relax
a little. Pills and wine made things easier.
As she drank, her pupils contracted
into dark points. "We should leave this country,"
she said on the long drive home. "The more foreign
travel, the worse it gets." Her words were slurred: smooth

stones at the bottom of a well. But her smooth
mouth twisted as she spoke. I kissed her. "Relax,"
I said. She said, "I'm shipping out to foreign
shores." Her crazy statements made things easier:
I went night-walking, soothed by the fresh country
air. My drumming heart felt uncontracted.

But coming back was more than I'd contracted
for. She lay unbreathing on the bed-- pale, smooth.
The doctor came, trained in another country.
He arranged things, but I still couldn't relax.
Her suicide note said it was easier
to die than live with me, that love was foreign

to my nature.... Life's contracted to one smooth
hope the next foreign country will be easier,
that I can finally grieve, finally relax.

HE DIVES TO FORGET THE ACCIDENT*

He dives, but dead girls will rise quickly to mind's
surfaces, like scrawled messages in bottles
gone overboard. Threadbare is the tie that binds

memory to a garbage bag, the rinds
of melon, six six-packs of empty bottles.
He dives, but dead girls will rise quickly to mind's

surfaces like bells. The starry night blinds
divers to love ink bleeding blue in bottles
gone overboard. Threadbare is the tie that binds

desire to the shore. The stellar clock winds
down, milk-faced girls crumble like pills in bottles.
He dives, but dead girls will rise quickly to mind's

surfaces. She laughed when she found new kinds
of sea glass-- milked-over fragments of bottles
gone overboard. Threadbare is the tie that binds

wounds. He drove, she sang, till "ninety-nine bottles"
crashed. Spilt-milk interns, upside-down bottles:
he dives, but dead girls will rise quickly to minds
gone overboard. Threadbare is the tie that binds.

in this "intensive" villanelle, a single word serves as the b rhyme throughout.

AFTER THE FUNERAL*

He follows his manifest breath back
to the frozen house he used to call home.
The second from the bottom step still
creaks, but the green porch swing is nowhere
to be seen. Regret, the black cat who never
liked men, winds around his legs, then moves away.

The key isn't scotch-taped to the back
of the ice-glazed mailbox. It's under the Home
Sweet Home mat he made in first grade, which is still
stained as if with faint green blood on the side where
he left boots... The key stalls... Why did he never
hang on to his all those times he moved away?

He's in... The tall clock stands at attention, back
to the wall-- Its case may be the dark home
of cornered spiders but the pendulum still
cuts a clean arc from here to nowhere
and back... The old deaf hound whose name he never
remembers has somehow found a way

to wedge herself between the wall and the back
of the couch, under his mother's childhood Home
Is Where the Heart Is sampler, which still
hangs by a thread. The dog's legs twitch-- She runs where
her dreams take her, fields where Brer Rabbit never
heard of Mr. Dog... He makes his slow way

to the bathroom closeted under the back
stairs-- He used to bring bottles of moonshine home
and hide them under this floor-- A friend joked, "Still
waters do run deep"-- But the kitchen's where
the warmest things happened. He never
sees deep bowls without remembering the way

the leaden dough would rise. He'd punch it back.
It always rose again. Things are coming home
to him too quickly. He goes outside. The still
night air is fresh and cold. He stands where
the lilacs were. The stars, which are never
just stars, shine. But not in the friendly way

they used to. He'll sell things and give the pets to
friends. Coming home still means being nowhere.
He'll never come back. He'll never get away.

this is a "bike lock" sestina: end words repeat in the same order throughout

DROWNING*

Swimming a strange lake... The unerring stroke
of arms is wrested from the unreflective cold--
palpable, dark... Tastes cleaner, deeper than love

ring my mouth as I wade to shore. The choke
of water loosens. Untested senses take hold:
swimming the strange lake, the unerring stroke

of arms, gets forgotten. Shedding the frayed cloak
of dawn, trees rise before me invested with mold,
palpable dark, tastes cleaner, deeper than love.

But glimpsed apparitions, the grinning folk
of folklore, herd me back to the watery fold.
Swimming the strange lake, the unerring stroke

of arms fails me: my breathing is the last joke
of creatures in league beneath me, older than old,
palpable, dark. Tastes cleaner, deeper than love

tempt me and I drown, shedding the wide yoke
of air... I surface among surfaces untold,
swimming a strange lake... The unerring stroke
of palpable dark tastes cleaner, deeper than love.

*this is a 'stand out' villanelle where one of the repeated end words does not
rhyme with anything else. The rhyme scheme begins a/b/c/ and ends a/b/a/c.

WHAT YOU GIVE ME*

You give me so much I don't want. To get you
to stop won't be easy. I don't think you'd try
to touch me, but if you ever did, I'd let you

know that wasn't called for. What does it net you
to give me books and wallets? I don't see why
you give me so much. I don't want to get you

angry, but your gifts unnerve me. I bet you
know that. You're smart, I think, and shy-- too shy
to touch me, but if you ever did, I'd let you

know it was wrong: issue the kind of threat you
understand, the kind that brings a tear to your eye.
You give me so much I don't want. To get you

to see what's happened as I do would set you
back some. There's a sanction you'd have to deny
to touch me, but if you ever did, I'd let you

know you'd transgressed. I felt when I met you
how it was, yet you gave me the slip, the lie.
You give me so much. I don't want to get you
to touch me, but if you ever did, I'd let you.

*in this "identical" villanelle, one word serves as the last word in all the "a"
rhymes: the rhyme comes in the verb: "let you," "get you," etc.

THE SHY MAN, THE FIREWORKS*

The once-dark garden where the shy man walks
is lit with torches, revealing a flickering
forest of strangers with drinks in their hands.
Green-eyed girls in silky sheaths
laugh and lick their crimson lips:
one tangles around his trembling legs.

Enormous flowers explode in the sky,
dazzle the shy man with falling crimson
that shrinks to a glow of green and is gone.
The shy man stands at the concrete edge
of a pool- the glassy surface shatters
when girl after laughing girl dives in.

At the wild splashing of the naked girls,
the shy man puts his hands in his pockets.
Their laughter blunts the edges of a long
denied desire and turns him crimson.
When a girl emerges wet and dripping,
he walks to her on feet of water.

He wraps her wetness in a towel;
they lie in the grass and he kisses her
on the soft outlines of her crimson lips.
A plane roars overhead. The girl
invades the wild forest of his body,
green for the taking. He feels a rush.
Hot flowers explode in a shining sky.

He awakes after dawn: the girl's feet
have slid between his shins like spoons.
His pants are a snake in the nearby grass.
He puts on his clothes and stumbles away,
pats himself down on the steps of a church.
He enters and kneels and asks for guidance.

His praying is like a blanket of snow
on the skeletal forest where his mind wanders.
He lights ranks of candles, kisses marble
feet: the once-dark naves turn
to familiar stone. Still, when he hears
the church bells ring, they ring with laughter.

*this was intended as a "skeletal" sestina lacking the customary repeated words
and envoi; adding an extra line to one of the stanzas was unintentional, but now
becomes part of the form*

BLIND HUNTER*

The photos leave him cold with regret, snowblind
with nostalgia... He stands with his nose against
the screen of memory. Through metal gauze, he takes
a look... His mother... A book called Cupid's Flight
lies in her lap. But love, like money, can't hold
her attention. The doctor says her mind

is going... He makes lunch. She tells him to mind
his manners. "If you touch yourself, you'll go blind,"
she says, then: "Mommy's hungry." He has to hold
her fork. Afterwards, he props her against
the railing, half-pushes her up the long flight
of stairs. They struggle toward the sun but she takes

her sweet time. "Your dad used a bow," she takes
this occasion to recall. "If he'd a mind
to shoot, he'd shoot. He could bring down geese in flight
so neat the V wouldn't break. Blind or no blind,
he'd bring geese home. And decoys were against
his principles. None of you boys can hold

a candle to him. He knew how to grab hold
of a bow. He had the heart and eye it takes
to shoot true... Sonny, don't hold my words against
me-- Some of his white lightning'll wipe your mind
clean." She's right, of course: Dawn finds him sitting, blind
drunk, at the window, watching the stars' white flight,

his dreams of crossbows, quarrels, a flight
of black swans. His mother falls from the sky: "Hold
me, I'm dying." "If I touch you, I'll go blind,"
he says. He buries her after several takes:
men rise to applaud the theatre of his mind...
All the next morning, she loses ground against

the forces of black and white. She sags against
him: "They must take coffins on a normal flight,"
he thinks. Then, "The quiver of my mind
is empty." Then, "I've got to get hold
of myself." He goes to the bathroom. He takes
two pills, comes back... Death is spreading like a blind

spot. She says, "A hunter, blind out of his mind,
against all reason, can't hold the bow right." As
level-headed as an arrow, she takes flight.

this is a run-on sestina. None of the lines are end-stopped until the final line

THE GREEN MAN*

He lived at the end of a dead-end
street. Farther on were woods he'd never seen
up close. When ordered out of a playmate's house
he stayed inside for weeks watching grass turn green
on the far side of the fence. Hands on the glass,
he spent alone the time that was his to spend.

His mother gave him an allowance to spend
on quick candy, during errands without end.
He bumped his forehead on the windshield glass
trying to point out things she hadn't seen,
like copper cables weather had turned green.
But errands without end ended at the house.

She gave him groceries to carry in the house.
Then he made himself scarce so she could spend
some time in the kitchen preparing fresh green
vegetables for the supper that would end
his day. At the table he tried to be seen
and not heard. He kept his eyes on his glass,

trying to make his glass-nose break. If his glass
was too full, he turned his plate into a house:
the knife would visit the fork– "I haven't seen
you in so long!"-- and bring his spoon-wife to spend
the night. Usually the fork would end
in bed between them, his head on a soft green

pillow... "How come you always leave your green
beans, sport?" His stepfather poured a glass
of wine. Sometimes such questions didn't end
even when all the lights in the house
were out. He'd hear his mom say, "Could you please spend
more time with him? He needs you. I haven't seen

him this withdrawn since his dad died." "Have you seen
him glare at me when I ask him about green
beans, for Christ's sake?" "I know, but could you spend
time with him tomorrow? Take him for a glass
of ginger ale, get him out of the house?"
Then came soft noises. Their talk was at an end.

Have you seen him grown up, a gardener who'll spend
hours with children? They tease him without end,
call him the green man, throw stones at his glass house.

another rhymed sestina (cf. "The Ending End")

45

OPIUM FIELDS IN TIME OF WAR*

Petals fall like blouses to the ground.
Sun rings in the Turkish morning like a bell.
Whole rows of women fall, without a sound,

to work, probing for the dust where dreams are found.
Their faith keeps them from using that they sell.
Petals fall like blouses to the ground.

Crowned with poppies is a small burial mound.
Soldiers killed the boy before he learned to spell.
Whole rows of women fall, without a sound,

to their knees. The air shakes with round after round
of gunfire. Soldiers rush through the poppies pell-mell.
Petals fall like blouses to the ground.

Somehow, Greek soldiers manage to surround
the field, swoop down on the women from a swell.
Whole rows of women fall, without a sound,

and soldiers full of the fury of hell
beat them and rape them. The soldiers groan and yell.
Blouses fall like petals to the ground.
Whole rows of women fall without a sound.

this is a couplet villanelle where a repeated phrase is reversed in the final stanza.

PART TWO:
FEMALE VOICES

ANOTHER LIFE*

Whatever I knew, I knew DAMNWELL.
Men bounced me till my mouth went dry.
I wishboned a horse and RODELIKEHELL.

Mom said there wasn't much to tell,
I'd bleed for years and then go dry.
Whatever I knew, I knew DAMNWELL.

When I was raped, she made me tell,
But I made sure my eyes were dry.
I wishboned a horse and RODELIKEHELL.

I married a boy who couldn't tell.
And I made sure I wasn't dry.
Whatever I knew, I knew DAMNWELL.

I didn't want kids and he could tell.
The day he left my eyes were dry.
I wishboned a horse and RODELIKEHELL.

The tree I hang from will never tell why:
The limb I hang from is stout, and dry:
Whatever I knew, I knew DAMNWELL:
I wishbone a horse and RIDELIKEHELL.

*another "present" sestina (cf. "This Gay Life") which changes tense in the final line.

51

HEARTS, FLOWERS

The heart only manages a small clutch.
Tiger lilies never pawed me. They clawed some
ordinary child. My mother couldn't touch

moonlight through glass; open windows meant too much
air. Cribbed by the dark, I sucked my honied thumb.
The heart only manages a small clutch.

At dusk, mother leaned against her rosewood hutch,
leaned like sunlight leans on lilacs or a dumb,
ordinary child. My mother couldn't touch

tulips without wanting more children: such
love, insistent on operations to plumb
the heart, only manages a small clutch.

My heart sprang a leak, testimony to Dutch
genes. Surgeons made me roll over, play a numb,
ordinary child. My mother couldn't touch

my heart or hive my brain's deciduous hum.
Look at me, bee drowning in chrysanthemum,
ordinary child my mother couldn't touch:
the heart only manages a small clutch.

103 Degrees

Daddy? Fever's got me. He wants me to keep
Sailing out to sea. But with your smile, you share
A secret. When I'm burning in my sleep,

You bring cool cloths. I awake-- and start to weep:
No one will ever care for me like you care,
Daddy... Fever's got me. He wants me to keep

Bloodying kleenex like delicate sheep--
He knows that under underwear, I wear
A secret. When I'm burning in my sleep,

Desert sun probes to the heart of a deep
Well: rattlers thicker than ropes lie coiled there.
Daddy? Fever's got me. He wants me to keep

Pushing head-sized boulders up a steep
Slope where vultures make everybody's nightmare
A secret. When I'm burning in my sleep,

Do you push aside my covers and stare?
Do you bend low to me and whiff my hair?
Daddy Fever's got me. He wants me to keep
A secret, when I'm burning in my sleep.

THE O OF LOVE

My mother said, "Let sexless angels stand guard."
Then, to me, "Make sure the outer door will close,
I want you to love me." And, again, "Hard

Times will come. Your private legs will be scarred,
Blood will film the ashen heart of the rose,"
My mother said. Let sexless angels stand guard.

I tried to speak, each word unearthed like a shard,
The O of love green and drooling like a hose.
"I want you to love me." And, again, hard

As it was (hosts of angels feathered and tarred),
I did with my lips whatever she chose.
My mother said, "Let sexless angels stand guard,

and spread your thin wings." "No pins have marred
This map," mother said. "Shut your eyes, try to doze,
I want you to love me." And again. Hard

Strokes stopped. When you touch me, I hear green: it grows
over her. Your mouth is stone on sharp words, those
my mother said... "*Let* sexless angels stand guard."
I want you to love me again, and hard.

STRANGER, FRIEND, FATHER

The moon touched her throat. She knew a knifing thrill
when a stranger took her arm, spoke of loss, love,
then nothing. His embrace left her cold. And still,

She took late walks alone, liking midnight's chill
reception. When the flagrant sun rose above
the moon, touched her throat, she knew a knifing thrill.

A friend's picnic supper on a heathered hill:
she watched clouds-- Saw a terrapin eat a dove,
then nothing. His embrace left her cold and still

he kept kissing her, laughed when she said he'd spill
her wine. In that night's dream, thumbs ordered to shove
the moon touched her throat. She knew a knifing thrill...

Lunch with her father-- Silence lay like a glove
on the floor between them. He said, You're dressed to kill,
then nothing. His embrace left her cold, and still,

she cried when he mentioned making out his will.
Death came riding, reined in the white horses of
the moon, touched her throat. She knew a knifing thrill,
then nothing. His embrace left her cold and still.

BURYING THE HATCHET

Mother? Lying stiff under mounded covers,
I once ate wafers, thinking God's flesh was bread.
I've buried the hatchet. In my lover's

eyes I saw New Jerusalem-- He said
he would love me until one of us was dead.
Mother? Lying stiff under mounded covers,

I used to hear your voice rasping in my head--
"Women are true Christians, broken and bled."
I've buried the hatchet.   In my lover's

arms, light as ash, I was carried to bed,
but we obeyed the Bible till we were wed.
Mother? Lying stiff under mounded covers

on my wedding night, I thought of you. He fed
me white cake crumbs till flesh-colored devils fled.
I've buried the hatchet. In my lover's

apartment, I look back at the clothes we've shed--
the eggshells we walk on, the water we tread--
Mother, lying stiff under mounded covers,
I've buried the hatchet in my lovers.

SHOCK
   for Tom

Tines of sunlight. No inoculations take
Effect ever after. Can bright switchmen heal
Someone here? Is a mirror that will break

Equal to the slide-- wet feet, tile? Does it make
The same noise as angels liquid in the steel
Tines of sunlight? No inoculations take

Away the slick ropes of twisted hair which snake
Down her back like the fingers of someone real
(Someone here is a mirror) that will break

Her neck. On gray days, she walks concrete, can fake
A smile. Till reddened clouds part like hair, reveal
Tines of sunlight. No inoculations take

Her hand when the light says go or help her bake
Gingerbread or tell her which ovens conceal
Someone. Here is the mirror that will break

Her heart. The dinner plate comes clean. She'll
Stab it, thinking-- What turns that round face piecemeal?
Tines of sunlight. No inoculations take.
Someone here is a mirror that will break.

Blood Oranges*

The therapist removed
his gaze. "Face your losses,
break them in small pieces,"
he told me. "Be precise.
Fight your fear. Make sharp
stabs at unfamiliar

things." He played familiar
the next time. He removed
his tie. But all his sharp
remarks about losses
cut me out-- His precise
lecture came in pieces.

He cut orange pieces.
They looked unfamiliar
cut in such small, precise
crescents. Then he removed
his watch. "Cut your losses,
girl," he said, in a sharp

tone. Then he took a sharp
knife to the red pieces.
He said, "Don't let losses
leave you unfamiliar
with good fruit." He removed
his fruit's skin with precise

motions. Mine weren't precise
till I picked up the sharp
knife. When I had removed
some of the red sections,
he played too familiar,
talking of his losses.

58

"Did you say your losses?"
I asked. "Be more precise.
Use common, familiar
words." I replied in sharp
remarks, strung in pieces,
to him… Then I removed

his clothes... His familiar
piece was precise: one sharp
thrust removed all losses.

this is a "sestinetta," a sestina where the lines are only six syllables long

THE EASY MIRACLE

You're skipping rope again. Everyone you know-
four, five-- is alive. Your Easter sister's home--
ninety-nine-- in time to see a miracle--
one hundred!-- But after that the easy
numbers return. Your mother saves you, knocking
on the window... Dinner!-- You take the steps

Noah-style... The kitchen's spotless. Your mom steps
forward gingerly to inspect you. You know
I don't allow dirt inside, she says, knocking
her spoon against the sink. This is a home,
not a stable... Wash up, I've saved the easy
chores for you. Dinner is not the miracle

it once was. Your sister says the miracle
of Easter is hogwash. Dad tells mom strong steps
should be taken. He calls Your sister "easy."
Your sister chokes. Your mom says, "Both of you know
I don't allow fights. Not here. Not at home."
Your sister: "Well, mom, at least I'm not knocking

the food." Later you go in without knocking.
Your sister frowns. "Don't wait for a miracle,
squirt," she says. "Miracles aren't allowed at home.
You'll have to get out, follow in my footsteps.
Life isn't just skipping a hundred, you know.
There are so many deaths, none of them easy."

Her eyes and flashing words make you uneasy.
You go to bed, start to sleep. There's a knocking.
Your father comes in, sits on the bed. "You know
we love each other," he says. "That's a miracle,
but sometimes your big sister oversteps
herself." He leans over, presses a kiss home...

lightning years-You tear yourself away from home
like tissue. Success doesn't come easy,
but it comes... You leave a loopy chain of steps
in someone's snow, ragged as your heart's knocking.
Every breath you manage is a miracle.
You survive, but what exactly do you know?

You know you'll go back-- You'll stand on the steps
knocking, hoping against hope for the easy
miracle-- Please, God, let no one be home.

BLUEGILL

Nothing matters much if you're lying,
but how many women do you dream about
in bed, beside me? It's a lot like flying

when I'm on my way to you-- The blue shying
away from common ground, the impulse to shout:
"Nothing matters if you're lying."

I'm awash-- A photo in a blue bath trying
to develop. How many succumb to doubt
in bed, beside me? It's a lot like flying,

making love. My inner child starts crying--
I ask aproned men for plums, but they're all out.
Nothing matters much if you're lying,

but I like the thought of blue fruit drying
in the sun. How many women thrash like trout
in bed, beside me? It's a lot like flying

for bluegill, this poem-- Metaphors aren't buying
me time, the bright stars are being put to rout.
Nothing matters much if you're lying
in bed beside me.... It's a lot like flying.

SOMETHING WE ALL DO

I'm not myself. Like a child in disguise,
I can't breathe right. Games aren't what's happening here,
Death is. Pulling the wool over mother's eyes

Was never easier. Visitors palm lies
Like stolen quarters, call her honey and dear--
I'm not myself. Like a child in disguise,

The sister hands out bags of goodies. She tries
For control, but medicine's not in charge here,
Death is. Pulling the wool over mother's eyes

Is something we all do. When the doctor pries
Her mouth open, I offer him a beer--
I'm not myself. Like a child in disguise,

My father shifts from foot to foot. He buys
Boxed negligees, but love's not spoken here,
Death is. Pulling the wool over mother's eyes

Is merciful. She stares up, coony with fear--
I hold her hands and the glassy truth comes clear--
I'm not myself. Like a child in disguise,
Death is pulling the wool over mother's eyes.

KNUCKLES*

She'd been left high and dry. She licked her lips, stocked
the fridge, cold humming hive, with knuckles. He knew
his way back to her. Opportunity knocked

just once-- She stood ready. White futures flocked
to her mind, gulls riding a tractor's wake. True,
she'd been left high and dry. She licked her lips, clocked

phantom planes. When she spoke of him, she knocked
on wood. Furrowed voices asked what they could do--
(She'd been left high and dry.) She licked her lips, shocked.

She was leaning on the ropes when liners docked--
let him parse her presence like a phrase, construe
his way back to her. Opportunity knocked

elsewhere, though. No notes. Nothing rocked her boat, rocked
her stalled horse, her wooden air. Couldn't he hew
his way back to her? Opportunity knocked

with brass knuckles. Wolves stood at the door and blew:
smart pigs laid on the trowel, made wolf-knuckle stew.
She'd been left high and dry. She licked her lips, blocked
his way back to her... Opportunity knocked.

*this is a "straightened" villanelle: the 1st line is repeated at the end of the
second and third tercets, then the 3rd line is repeated at the end of the fourth and
fifth, instead of in the normal alteration

THE ARTWORK ON THE BACKS OF GARGOYLES*

Black wood strips, wire x's-- Now the old
veranda is a screened in porch. "I've never
seen a man so stuck on himself," his sister
says loudly. "He thinks I'm hot to marry
him... And does he ask himself why anyone
would want him? No. He's too busy handing out

bachelor medals." She tucks her long legs up and
turns toward him, locket face flushed. "I'll never
see him again. I'm like his sister,
he says, and he doesn't want to marry
his sister... But, hell, why should anyone
listen to this, even a brother fresh out

of the seminary? Tell your big sister --
why not stay here tomorrow, and milk the old
prodigal bit? Why should any man marry
himself to books the way you do? You've never
even been drunk! They'll think you're a weak sister,
those boys you're going to reform. They'll be out

to get you. A little debauchery and
sex wouldn't hurt you." Silence. "Does anyone
else talk so wicked to you? I'll make you old
before your time." Silence. "Better to marry
than burn, your Bible says. So how come you and
I are so hot to the touch? I should get out

of here, I guess." Long silence. "I'm your sister,
for God's sake. Those times in the shed, I never
meant to mess us up. I know you know that, and
yet, even now, your eyes are full of the old
reproaches. Christ, the stars are really out
in force tonight... I almost think anyone

can be happy, even those who don't marry-
don't or can't. God, don't you smile at anyone
anymore? That's better. Give me the old
razzle-dazzle. Remember Jen? She'd never
seen such a beautiful boy, she said. And
mother got rid of her-- Told her to get out.

And Jennie said, 'It ain't me, it's his sister
you need to watch....' All these years and I've never
forgotten. I saw the way she held you and
kissed you. At first I was shocked that anyone,
any grownup, was like that. I asked how old
she was once. You said, 'Old enough to marry.'

You'd never tell anyone- Your wife, if you
marry- what your sister...? No, you go ahead.
I'll lock up, make sure the lights are out."

*this is a "septina": It has seven repeated words, one of which drops out of each
stanza. In this septina, each line-ending word represents one of the seven parts of
speech.

To Her Husband, To Her Lover

Some story-wife crystallizes in salt
when she looks back. I count knots in boards, or crumbs
when you touch me sometimes. It's not my fault

Lightning strikes one like a clock in the hall.
thought-kids play musical chairs: your wife becomes
some story-wife, crystallizes in salt,

dissolves. If I drink from your cup, it will fall,
break on honeycombed tile. An inside girl hums
when you touch me sometimes. It's not my fault

I get thrown-- clay bowl, horseless rider, striped ball
rolling uphill... When cornered Jack is all thumbs,
some story-wife crystallizes in salt,

licks him like a stamp.   The icebox opens, all
edibles dance, disingenuous as plums,
when you touch me sometimes.   It's not my fault

I shed husbands like needles. Each new snow numbs
April's green brink, and your eyes scare me like drums.
Some story-wife crystallizes in salt
when you touch me... Sometimes, it's not my fault.

RAPUNZEL

Lost in long separateness, I sometimes forget
where I am. The witch's minions stand sentry
at every open window. Is a threat

posed by flickering skies in a kind of wet
nightmare not to be taken seriously?
Lost in long separateness, I sometimes forget.

There may be no blue numbers on my arm, yet
the storm is closing in. There's a black Nazi
at every open window. Is a threat

like a wicked fisherman, dragging his net
through the mackerel-rich but salt-encumbered sea?
Lost in long separateness, I sometimes forget

who I am. What good did it do to let
my hair down? I wanted to jump and go free
at every open window. Is a threat

what brought you? Did you climb on a kind of bet?
Never mind. Wrap your subtle arms around me.
Lost in long togetherness, we might forget
that every window is an open threat.

AN OLD CRECHE*

I look inside and count my blessings like sheep--
Mary, Joseph, the wise men are all there, but
there is no child. I can afford to keep

looking for another. God's words can sleep
in kisses: the mouths of children burn me but
I look inside and count my blessings like sheep.

When the sign says Walk, women of plenty beep
brass horns. My carriage springs bob like apples, but
there is no child. I can afford to keep

prowling moon beaches. Unseen sea horses leap
open-mouthed, dash me against sticks and stones.
I look inside and count my blessings like sheep.

Our sawed-off tree, moated, bristles with a heap
of tied-up boxes and wind-up dolls, but
there is no child. I can afford to keep

the coil of Eden hidden. I know what
green things wombs are. Unsprung seeds make me weep.
I look inside and count my blessings like sheep:
there is no child I can afford to keep.

   *this is an irregular villanelle

EASY CONJUNCTIONS*

The moon looks in no one's mirror but
her own. She espouses easy conjunctions,
intent on equating the green push and
pull that roughens the oceans with melons or
the puckering membrane that divides
the pregnant woman from her child. She can't stand

all the talk about moods and symptoms, can't stand
the way men appropriate her schedule, but
who can fault her bright conundrums? She divides
the sky, scimitars its darker junctions
by dancing on her mother's grave. Or
veils her light in a widow's wandering and

weeds. Who can deny the moon what she wants? And
who can say what that is? She lets no one stand
in her way with weak-kneed objections or
qualms on hot nights-- The palms may bow and scrape but
she pays no attention, forcing conjunction
to the point of consequence so cell divides

from cell... Now, the docile belly divides,
yields a premature child to his mother and
her green surgeon. The father has no function--
he waits in the waiting room, then goes to stand
like a forked stick in the men's room, but
can't produce anything more. The moon or

a pale look-alike drifts past: his mother or
a young nurse he knows, whose dream-breasts he divides
with target circles. Water wets his chin but
the cry of gulls is the pay phone ringing and
he's still alone in the men's room-- Now he'll stand
near the mirror and shave, foam like an unction.

On the ward, a priest gives her extreme unction:
the new mother needs to die, or
soon will-- that's what she starts to understand,
tired of being a land a knife divides,
where breasts are explosive devices, and
someone keeps stripping her like a mine. But

she stands where time divides, ready to protest
the last injunction. But, ready or not, words
are gone. She's left with silence, and the moon.

this is a "conjunctive" sestina- featuring "but," "and," and "or."

BACK NORTH

Days whiz by like beads or boxcars. I lost track
of barred crossings, suckled by the Georgia stall
of everything, myself included. I'm back

where birch goes begging like altered brides, and black
willows gainsay white hopes, downcast widows all.
Days whiz by like beads or boxcars. I lost track

of green-bladed pockets, dimes rich with the smack
of palmers. Cats' cradles nipped the budding fall
of everything, myself included: I'm back

where dusk used to slide home as if at the crack
of a bat, the white arc of an uncaught ball.
Days whiz by like beads or boxcars. I lost track

of undershirted girls who taught me the knack
of two-fingered groping in the crumbling wall
of everything, myself included. I'm back

to back, dueling the woman in white. Nuns call
old prescriptions from their station down the hall.
Days whiz by like beads or boxcars. I lost track
of everything, myself included. I'm back.

PART TWO:
CODA
GENDER-FLUID VOICES

INTRO TO LIT:*
  for Judith Dewoskin

8:00 a.m. Guest-teaching English at the high school.
A cornered girl, scribbling. I had asked
the kids to hand in "a line of poetry;"
she balled up three pages before she could give
me one. Almost nothing managed to survive
her strict self-censorship: all the words

had been crossed out except the word, "words.
"Words" sat cornered on the page, high
and dry, like the fruit powders I survive
on in winter, mixed with water. Had I asked
too much? Had I challenged her to give
me more than she could? Or was "poetry"

the problem? Had home or school brought poetry
to its knees, pounded truth and beauty till words
were all that was left? What could I give
this cornered girl to make her see the high
drama of the classroom now? What if I asked
her which words she needed to survive?

The class was staring at me. Would they survive
the hour? Would I? A march of poetry
began in my brain, led by a masked
priest, chanting Anglo-Saxon words like "thu," words
that were saddled donkeys bringing God's high
purpose to us before local dogs could give

chase. But quoting the old poets might give
these back-packed kids the wrong idea. To survive
their silent scrutiny I needed both high
craft and current lingo, a poetry
written in their vernacular: wolf-words
wrapped in fleece, that trotted to them masked

as clouds with legs, lullaby lambs. I'd asked
the class to write lines of poetry, to give
me fuel, but now I needed to take their words,
make of them a poem to help us all survive.
I would prove to them, prove to myself, that high
poetry was now. They were that poetry.

In response to unasked questions, I'd give
them back their words alive- and sound the high
summons of poetry, thought letting beauty survive...

P.S. That's what happened, but I was the student,
and the word I wrote on my paper was "truth."
You that are cornered in classrooms- uncrumple
your fists, speak the inside truth. We need to hear
what you need to say, and life, like this poem, is
sometimes not over quite as soon as you think.

this is a "sestina plus" that adds a final sestet after the envoi

THE LAW, BEAUTY, NAKEDNESS, RELIGION*
  for Jim Lounsbury

I sit behind you at the edge of light
watching you paint. Outside, rain is falling on
the just and unjust, but your studio is
a world apart from rain or cold religion,
slick expressways, soaked pedestrians. Your face
is the dark side of a lovers' moon as your

canvas nude commands you, though the jut of your
jaw tells me what a battleground of light
and dark the two of you struggle in. Her face
stays toward me, her eyes keep falling on
me-- A real woman, fully clothed. Religion,
if I had one, would give me that look: she is

calm beyond indolence. Her muscled thigh is
what first betrays her. As determined as your
jaw, the curve of her leg is a religion
unto itself, and her velvet V makes light
of other darks. Soldiers who spend themselves on
such darkness in the dark, will find themselves face

down in such lush undergrowth, they have to face
ultimates. If they come home, such is
that power, they could spend their lives falling on
the marriage bed, dizzy with gratitude. "Your
body was my star," they'll tell their wives. "A light
from beyond the zones of war, the religion

of death." They will not be lying-- Religion
will surround them in the bedroom. The first face
they see in Saturday morning's lavish light
will be God's face. Such is the law. Such, too, is
beauty, nakedness, rebellion, your
insolent nude... Outside, rain is falling on

houses indiscriminately, falling on
streets as randomly as blissful religion.
Oh, and now-- now, you are turning toward me. Your
eyes are seeking me out. We are face to face.
The sacred comes with its own rush. Love is
the shadow cast here, now, by that other light.

On your face, random light is falling like religion.

this is a sestina that ends by putting all the repeated words in one sentence.

DYING IN THE HOSPITAL
for K.R.

You lie mute, and don't manage to look at me.
You look at me, and don't manage to lie mute.
You try to disappear like a stone in the lake outside.
Like a stone in the lake outside, you try to disappear.
You lie mute, and manage to look at the lake outside.
You don't try to disappear in me like a stone.

I am sure of nothing in this place, and feelings of love don't belong.
Feelings of love don't belong in this place, and I am sure of nothing.
Since I know nothing at all, it's best not to speak of love to me.
It's best not to speak at all to me, since I know nothing of love.
Since I know feelings of love don't belong in this place, and I am
sure of nothing, nothing at all, it's best not to speak of love to me.

Nothing means anything to me now; we are a bell without sound.
We are a bell without sound now; nothing means anything to me.
I'm sorry you're dying. If only I could tell you.
If only I could tell you I'm sorry you're dying.
Nothing means anything. I'm only sorry you're dying without me.
If I could tell you we are a bell to sound now.

You try to sound like a bell, and tell me to look at the lake
outside. I don't. Since I know feelings of love don't belong to me,
and am sure of nothing in this place, nothing at all, it's best
not to speak now. You lie mute. Nothing means anything without
you. If only I could manage to disappear. You're
a stone of love in me: I'm sorry we are dying.

A WIDOW/ER

You slide into daylight— running out of love
and breath in dreams where you knew how to get home.
Everything will stay exactly as it is
until you have to put your thoughts into words…
You shower and select your clothes, taking
small liberties with the similes you wear.

You group pieces of your jigsaw life where
you can. Yesterday's worries are coming
back to you, like raucous crows. After taking
out the trash, you leave your split level home
and drive off to do work you don't love,
or like, or value, because what you do is

who you were, not who you are… <u>Work</u>. The clock is
a relentless sun, a coin from fires where
men and women are consumed, where they twist love
to a joke that ends with the second coming.
You get takeout from a counter known for home
cooking, and eat at your desk. Now you're taking

too long or not long enough. Someone's taking
you on, or down, or over, and seeing is
believing the worst…. When it's dark; you go home--
freeway lights in the rain blur to a tale where
those who are good and ready, get what's coming
to them… When you were young, you used to think love

was like the dove in magic acts; later, love
turned to a pigeon in the park, taking
bread from your hand; now it's God's dove, coming
back to the ark without a branch--which is
God's way of saying there are no places where
His anger hasn't reached: there is no home

left to go to…. Traffic thins. You're almost home.
You let yourself in, imagining love
as a pair of your beloved's boots right where
they should be— by the door. Without taking
off your coat, you flood the room with light. This is
where your no-longer-dead spouse says, "Coming."

And now fantasy stuns you: you're both home.
Love is for the making; you both think you know
what's coming... God hasn't yet started taking.

THE GROUND IS FROZEN

I ask myself useless questions. Why
Aren't you here? Why am I? I go to the door.
I know there's nothing. Pain can't be measured by

Audible clocks. Is that the reason I
Count the strokes it takes to wax the kitchen floor?
I ask myself useless questions. Why

Has it come to this? I open what is my
Closet now, hoping for skeletons galore.
I know there's nothing. Pain can't be measured by

Sport coats or blouses or suits hung high and dry.
Who barbed the staves in the celestial score?
I ask myself useless questions. Why

Do I fear God in the buzzing of a fly?
You died with your eyes open. looking for more.
I know there's nothing. Pain can't be measured by

Thrift-shop boxes. Will I learn to ignore
Men in vans who dance off with the clothes you wore?
I ask myself useless questions. Why?
I know there's nothing pain can't be measured by.

GOD'S CHILDREN*

Old suggestions are knives planted in my round
stupid heart, whose dull beating never ceases.
Body embedded in honeysuckled ground,

the moon floats lightly on the lake where you drowned.
You climb toward me in grassy exegesis.
Old suggestions are knives planted in my round

belly... You were swollen by the time they found
you, a Buddha of watery releases.
Body embedded in honeysuckled ground,

stones are God's children. Their sinkings astound
us, leave us cold. Our need for air increases.
Old suggestions are knives planted in my round

breasts, my rounder mouth. I didn't make a sound
when your cold fingers tore my mind to pieces.
Body embedded in honeysuckled ground,

my love, it costs me nothing more to end my life.
Old suggestions are knives planted in my round
body. Embedded in honeysuckled ground,
our ashes will mingle us as man and wife.

*this is an "altered" villanelle, embedding the final coming together of lines 1
and 3 within the final stanza, instead of placing the two lines at the end*

I GIVE MYSELF

I give myself to you like water. You're
trembling, strung to the pulse of what could be
the breath I breathe. The moon's slow ocean, the shore,

keep us true. When he of broken windows, more
child than ghost, twists me at night like the wrong key,
I give myself to you. Like water, your

desires run underground, rise to score
hills with the sweet stress of long releasing, free
the breath I breathe. The moon's slow ocean, the shore

were implicit in our first embrace. For
I alone kiss you where you bend-- elbow, knee.
I give myself to you like water. You're

mesquite smoke on my fingers, the door
I know will open, the dark where I see
the breath I breathe. The moon's slow ocean, the shore,

stretch to the end of ending when you touch me.
Silence shades us, branched and rooted as a tree:
I give myself to you like water. You're
the breath I breathe, the moon's slow ocean, the shore.

PARADELLE ON LOVE

Once, our hearts were open. We made love.
We made love once our hearts were open.
We turned and embraced in huge, unmade spaces ruined by war.
Unmade, we turned and embraced in huge spaces ruined by war.
Once we turned and embraced open war in huge spaces we made,
our hearts were ruined by unmade love.

Have you vanished from the face of this life?
You have vanished from the face of this life.
Still, I miss belonging to you and longing to have love.
Still, I miss belonging to you to have love and longing.
I have vanished from this life to miss longing,
and still you have the face of love belonging to you.

Our old blind pain did not help us find a way to God.
Our old pain did not help us find a way to blind God.
God could not let us be true to one another.
One God could not let us be true to another.
Let us find another blind God to be true to.
Our old one way pain God did not, could not help us.

Our old way of belonging to blind war turned our
hearts' spaces to pain. We once embraced love, and
could have vanished from another God, to find
the one true face to help us. You were not open, God.
You did not let be, and have ruined us. And, still, in
this unmade life made huge by longing, I miss love.

WHERE I STAND*

I stand by high windows. Something pushes me,
But I think of you and turn from death to sleep.
Your face is always the last face I see

Before I drop off. Small dream-people weep
Tears of fire as their relatives leap.
I stand by high windows. Something pushes me,

And I jump, falling past the face of a steep
Cliff, along with clouds and sacrificial sheep.
Your face is always the last face I see.

I awake in the long, small hours, deep
In hurt nerves. I have sewn what I can't reap--
I stand by high windows. Something pushes me,

But dawn is real. People are starting to creep
About on the street. I turn to you, "Please, keep
Me safe." But you're not there. "Tomorrow, we

Could meet," you said. I said I wasn't free.
I stand by high windows. Something pushes me.
Your face, for always, is the last face I see.

*this is a truncated sestina, where the final stanza eliminates the "b" rhyme and is a tercet rhymed a/a/a.

A DOOR THAT DOESN'T EXIST*

Inches beyond your door, a late spring rain
is falling. Always, when I am with you,
it is spring, and raining. I shiver, and see
the red curtains you brought from India move
in the wind. It is cold, but your door
is open. When I am with you, you always

keep the door open, and it is always
cold. The rain on your roof doesn't sound like rain
but a host of kids sing-songing, "Close the door,
they're coming in the window." I'm glad you
don't hear. I'm glad that your clouds can move
across your sky, unburdened by the storms I see

in the gray and fraying clouds. But when I see
you dazzle your canvas with green, I always
want to live in your landscapes. I want to move
through hills that rise like music and fall like rain.
I want to build a barn to match the fields you
paint, but I sit still, staring at a door

which would be white if it existed, a door
that discloses nothing but blue. Your birds see
past the threshold of the visible- Yet you
brush them, too, into corners. And, always,
because it sounds like pounding children, the rain
makes me think I exist at one remove

from everything. I don't know why your fields move
me so much, or why it hurts me that your door
stays open. Or why rain that isn't your rain
frightens me. Or why no one else seems to see
angels swimming in your skies, but I'll always
feel at home in the abandoned landscapes you

create, among the whirling dervish trees you
scatter like baby dragons' teeth. When you move
the chair I sit on to watch you, you always
move it close to the corner, nearer the door,
sandwiching me between my need to see
and my fear of the cold, inquisitive rain.

But when I see you paint, a door in me
always opens. Rain turns the outside world
quicksilver, and I feel no need to move.

this is a run-on sestina manqué where there is only one end-stopped line in the body of the poem, just before the envoi

Ned's Aria

Beginnings, yes. But who knows how things will end?
As a feverish child, singing in my everyday sickbed,
I didn't. Neither did my seamstress mother, forced to bend
every night over her own lap, biting off thread
as she sewed. She said, "The truth isn't in wine,
or song. If you want the truth, you have to divine

it like underground water, with a stick, not try to define
it as yours, but the one truth worth knowing, we learn at the end."
My Sunday school teachers didn't confine
themselves to the truth: "Sing at the table, sing in bed,"
they told me. "The Devil will get you when you're dead."
They really thought-- I thought, as well-- God would send

singers of love songs to hell. But my path there took a sudden bend
in high school, when my art teacher praised "the Romantic, divine
Fragonard..." She said Classicism was hanging by a thread,
his swinging girl, her half-off shoe, marked its end.
I hung a poster of that girl above my bed:
I could almost hear her singing. Some nights, I'd dream her fine

blue day, her lover, her after-world, were mine--
I'd swing into heaven on a song! But that dream would end
in daylight guilt, my covers at the foot of my bed…
Mom said "You need dates, Lynn— a cocktail party line."
Her words wandered. When she finally found the deep end
of her life, her mind bent over, and bit off the thread

of her thought. Ned, my college voice coach, said
"You're hopeless. I love you." Ned drank too much wine,
but he wove my name into an aria. He became my friend,
my confidante, my lover. The school year came to an end,
and Ned had no job. He got drunk and enlisted one fine
May day— Nine months later, his last letter home said

"Music obscures the truth."   When I'm lying in bed
some nights, the aria Ned rewrote for me starts to thread
its way through the dark of my mind like a musical vine.
The ticking clock is a metronome, then, not a mine.
I hear his love song coming from beyond the bend,
"Credi-mi Lynn-ben, Credi-mi al-men."

A sword hangs by a thread above the bed
I call mine. I hope our spirits will blend into mercy
like music at the end: it's a hope I savor like wine.

MOTHER'S NOTE HOME

Of all the dog-eared scrapbook's mysteries, she
draws your attention, young and lovely and dark
in the arms of a stranger. Something, the light
or the man, frays her composure. She must know
your father– her one note home seems to describe
him-- but he is not the man who embraces

her here. Your mother never liked frank embraces
such as this; it must have offended her, she
who was so private even you can't describe
her with conviction. She held true to the dark
side of her own life, and most of what you know,
you know through remembrances which came to light

only after her death. She could play "The Flight
of the Bumblebee." She never wore braces.
She had a pony she rode side-saddle. No
one in sixth grade had better penmanship. She
discovered art in high school, and wrote dark
poems with no misspellings trying to describe

love. In college, she stopped trying to describe
anything, rewrote "Sleeping Beauty," made light
of love. Her prince is totally in the dark--
when he kisses Beauty, he tastes the traces
of poison on her lips, and they both die... She
left college in her senior year for no

good reason. For years, then, there was nothing-- No
notes or pictures except the one to describe
what must have happened. But with your birth, she
returned. On a stiff white card, she drew a light
bulb, your name and weight, and picked up the traces
of her life. There follows a series of dark

snapshots: you as infant, toddler, Scout (the dark
one on the end). High School. College. Grad school. No
heart-tugs in these, just seas of frozen faces,
till the last. You see you, starting to inscribe
a book of poems under a bookstore spotlight.
Your mother's not in these pictures because she

took them. But your poems explore longings she lived,
and she taught you the one principle you know:
whatever light describes, the dark embraces.

Publisher's Note about the Book

In 2019, Lyn and I featured for *lastbench little magazine* and Antivirus Publications at New York City Poetry Festival.

Lyn's most important work is celebrated internationally. She is well traveled and her poetry is also a traveler. She has many published works and has been praised by some of the most prominent literary voices. However, her work has not yet captured a mainstream audience.

We at Transcendent Zero Press are proud to bring this offering of poetry worth celebrating from a master poet to the reader.

Dustin Pickering

About the Author

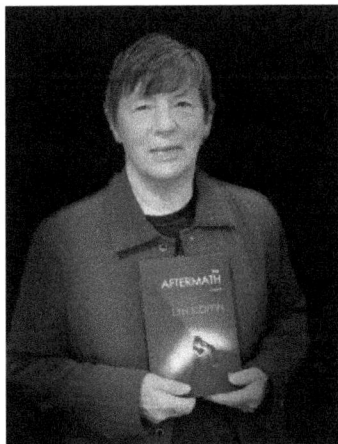

Lyn is a widely published author, with over 30 books published by Doubleday, Ithaca House, Abattoir Editions and others. Lyn was Asssistant Editor of the Michigan Quarterly Review and taught at the University of Michigan, The University of Detroit, The University of Milwaukee and the Milwaukee Institute of Art and Design. She has won many awards. Her youtube channel (Lyn Coffin) features some of her plays, her lectures, and her bi-weekly series on "Notable Nonagenarians." One of her short fictions was selected by Joyce Carol Oates for Best American Short Stories. Her novel The Aftermath (Adelaide Books, 2020) is available on Amazon and has received strongly positive reviews. One of her essays appears in a book of scholarly essays edited by William Barillas: A Field Guide to Theodore Roethke, 2020. Her translation of Shota Rustaveli's *The Knight in the Panther Skin* won the country of Georgia's SABA Prize.

About the Photographer

All photos featured in *Artwork on the Backs of Gargoyles* are by Walt Halperin. Walt Halperin was born in San Jose, California, grew up in New England, attended Brown University and is currently Professor Emeritus in the Biology Dept at the University of Washington. Walt's wife is an Art Historian and he has traveled widely with her, viewing and photographing Romanesque churches all over Europe.

Walter writes: "In Salamanca one of the university buildings has finely carved panels of a type known as 'plateresque'. There was some damage over the centuries and when the modern stone masons did some repairs, they put in a few jokes. The photo that marks the Gender Fluid section shows one such joke: a figure in a space suit (74). Another joke is a gargoyle holding an ice cream cone: see my photo on the following page."

www.ingramcontent.com/pod-product-compliance
Lightning Source LLC
Chambersburg PA
CBHW051432090426
42737CB00014B/2931